Call to Love

In the Rose Garden with Rumi

Call to Love

In the Rose Garden with Rumi

JELALUDDIN RUMI

TRANSLATED AND EDITED BY ANDREW HARVEY

PHOTOGRAPHS BY LEKHA SINGH

STERLING

New York / London
www.sterlingpublishing.com

Library of Congress Cataloging-in-Publication Data Is Available

2 4 6 8 10 9 7 5 3 1

Published by Sterling Publishing Co., Inc.
387 Park Avenue South, New York, NY 10016
Translation © 2007 by Andrew Harvey
Photography © 2007 by Lekha Singh
Distributed in Canada by Sterling Publishing
c/o Canadian Manda Group, 165 Dufferin Street
Toronto, Ontario, Canada M6K 3H6
Distributed in the United Kingdom by GMC Distribution Services
Castle Place, 166 High Street, Lewes, East Sussex, England BN7 1XU
Distributed in Australia by Capricorn Link (Australia) Pty. Ltd.
P.O. Box 704, Windsor, NSW 2756, Australia

Sterling ISBN-13: 978-1-4027-4510-2
ISBN-10: 1-4027-4510-9

For information about custom editions, special sales, premium and
corporate purchases, please contact Sterling Special Sales
Department at 800-805-5489 or specialsales@sterlingpub.com.

PREFACE

Imagine a being with the soul force and vision of a Christ or Buddha, the philosophical intellect of a Plato, and the extravagant literary gifts of a Shakespeare and you begin to understand who Rumi was, and is. This Persian mystical poet who lived in Turkey in the thirteenth century loved, prayed, and wrote in a civilization very different from ours; yet he is now the most widely read poet in the United States, cherished by millions of people of all religious affiliations and quoted by politicians, sportsmen, film stars, and social activists as well as seekers and spiritual teachers. Rumi has always been loved in the East (his epic, the *Mathnawi*, has been considered second only to the Koran in holiness and popularity); now he is revered everywhere in the West. Once, on a crowded New York City subway in the early morning, I counted five people reading him in different versions—including a passionate adolescent boy with pimples and a dramatic red scarf flung around his neck, a long-legged, white-faced girl on her way to ballet class, and an old African-American woman in shabby clothes sitting next to me whose eyes were brilliant with tears. I turned to the old woman and asked her what she saw in Rumi. "He knows everything about love," she said. "All the suffering, all the ecstasy, all the beauty."

The simplicity of her words, and the authority with which she delivered them, her voice rising and trembling like a Baptist preacher's, have haunted me ever since. Rumi does indeed know everything about the suffering, ecstasy, and beauty of love; his own terrifying and sublime relationship with his heart-friend and spiritual teacher Shams of Tabriz opened for him, as he wrote, "the whole universe of passion." It is this "universe of passion" and the revelations it gave him of the burning and glorious presence of God that illumined his poetry and made it naked and poignant, something an adolescent boy or girl can be shaken by, as well as an old woman with a lifetime's profound experience behind her.

The Sufi tradition that Rumi drew his deepest inspiration from worked with a few key images for centuries—images whose meanings and possibilities of suggestion were, seemingly, boundless. Chief among these were "rose" and "rose garden." For the Sufi, "rose" and "rose garden" are symbols with multiple meanings, all of which are implied whenever the words are used. For example, the image of the rose could evoke at once a high spiritual state, a visionary ecstasy, an inspiration, and the Rose that is the universe. As for the image of the rose garden, it embraces at once all the glories of the created world and all the visionary splendors of the awakened heart that sees the perfection of God's handiwork appearing in all things and events. In his book "Table-talk," Rumi writes, "When grace wills, you will know this world to be the Rose Garden of rose gardens, a paradise where nothing is ever born and nothing ever dies. You will realize that you and its Gardener are one heart, one breath. This is the heaven the Beloved keeps for the lovers; no one arrives in it who has not been through ring after ring of fire."

The poems and images we have gathered together and shaped here work with this full, rich range of meanings. Dostoyevsky, the great Russian writer, whose sense of divine passion and presence matched Rumi's, once wrote: "The world will be saved by Beauty." The "Beauty" he was speaking of was, of course, far more than a physical or even a natural loveliness; it was a radiant quality of the heart, a sense of the inner magnificence of the soul as reflected in artistic creation. This kind of "Beauty" has never been more needed than it is now, in our seedy, dangerous, despairing time, for it gives hope, renews our joy of being human and divine, fills us with the passion to love and serve more abandonedly, makes us fervent and resilient in the face of trauma and catastrophe. Even the agony of love that Rumi knew and speaks of so eloquently is one that is luminous with this "Beauty" because it does not simply devastate, but transforms.

We hope this book of ours invites you into a rose garden you can wander in both drunkenly and lucidly. May its sumptuousness inspire you, and may its perfumes awaken you to passionate life.

—Andrew Harvey
—Lekha Singh

For my mother,
Kathleen Elizabeth Harvey,
who goes on teaching me about courage

—ANDREW

For my father, Pratap Singh,
for his love of poetry

—LEKHA

Come, the rose garden
has flowered . . .

It is the time of resurrection,
the time of eternity.
It is the time of generosity,
the sea of lavish splendor.
The treasure of gifts has come,
its shining has flamed out.
See, the rose garden of love
is rising from the world's agony.

Each moment from all sides rushes to us the call to love.

We are running to contemplate its vast green field.

Do you want to come with us?

This is not the time to stay at home,

but to go out and give yourself to the rose garden.

The dawn of joy has arisen,

and this is the moment of vision.

In all the worlds and heavens
not a bird moves a wing
not a straw trembles
but by God's eternal law.
No one can explain this
and no one should try.
Who can number the roses
in the Almighty's rose garden?
How could the Beloved be
snared in a net of words?

Just this morning,
contemplation
led me into
the rose garden that is
neither
outside this world
nor within it.

Garden of miracles,
what kind of garden are you?

A garden
neither autumn nor winter
makes afraid.

Love is the infinite rose garden;
Eternal Life the least of its blooms.

*What was whispered to the rose to break it open
last night was whispered to my heart.*

Love, you have created us
with thirsty hearts
and bound us fast
to the Source of Splendor.
For you, my thorns have blossomed,
my atoms exploded into suns!

There is no salvation for the soul
but to fall in love.
Only lovers can escape
out of these two worlds.
This was ordained in creation.
Only from the heart
can you reach the sky:
The Rose of Glory
can grow only from the heart.

Silence you are the diamond in me
the Jewel of my real wealth!
From your soft earth
grow thousands of rose gardens
whose perfumes drown me in my heart.

There comes a holy and transparent time
when every touch of beauty
opens the heart to tears.
This is the time the Beloved of heaven
is brought tenderly on earth.
This is the time of the opening of the rose.

—*Hazrat Inayat Khan*

You
who are absent there
we have found you here

in this Rose of Splendor.

You are non-existent
as essence—
yet you exist

in this unfolding Light-Flower.

—*Jili*

Before a flower can open in the rose garden
thousands of thorns come to pierce it.
Although the soul has received only grief.
Love has made her turn away from the world:
Look for the ecstasy of a lover of God—
all the joys of this world lie at its feet.

Misery and joy

have the same

shape in this world:

You may call the

rose an open

heart or a

broken heart.

—*Dard*

Love drives you mad
from revelation to revelation
through ordeal after ordeal
until humble and broken
you are carried tenderly
into the heart of the rose.

When the Invisible has become your food,
you've won Eternal Life and death has fled.
When the agony of love has begun to expand your life,
roses and lilacs take over the garden of your soul.

You're a fish in the trap of the body;
look at the fisherman, don't look at the net.
Gaze in wonder at the infinite rose garden,
don't consider that thorn that wounded your foot.
Contemplate the Bird of Heaven whose shadow shelters you,
don't look at the crow that escaped your hands.
Put your trust in Him who gives life and ecstasy;
don't mourn what doesn't exist, cling to what does.

While the image of the Beloved burns in our heart
the whole of life flows in contemplation.
Wherever union with the Beloved exists
there is, in the middle of the house,
a flowering rose garden.

I burnish bright the mirror of my heart
until at last, reflected for my rapture,
the Self's eternal beauty appears.

If you think of the rose,
you will become the rose.
If you think of the nightingale,
you will become the nightingale.

You are a drop:
Divine Being is the ocean.
While you still live,
hold steadily before you
the vision of the whole
and you will be the whole.

—Zeb-un-nisa

Through love bitter things seem sweet.

Through love scraps of copper are turned to gold.

Through love dregs taste like clear wine.

Through love agonies are healing balms.

Through love thorns become roses.

Through love vinegar becomes rich wine.

Through love the scaffold becomes a throne.

Through love disaster becomes good fortune.

Through love a prison becomes a rose garden.

Through love burning fire is a fragrant light.

Through love the devil becomes an angel.

Through love stones become soft as butter.

Through love grief is like delight.

Through love demons become servants of God.

Through love stings are like honey.

Through love lions are harmless as mice.

Through love sickness is health.

Through love the dead are resurrected.

Through love the emperor becomes a slave.

The soul's extravagance is endless.
 Spring after spring after spring . . .
  We are your gardens dying, blossoming.

In the center of the rose
a diamond burns forever
larger than all the worlds
more brilliant than any sun.
In the Divine Heart
of the Beloved
Infinite Passion arises in
Infinite Peace.

Lovers know there are roses
in the bloody veil of love;
they live astounded
by Love's matchless beauty.
The intellect says,
"The six directions are blocked!"
Love says, "There's a way!
I've taken it thousands of times."
Intellect sees a market
and starts to haggle;
Love sees thousands of markets
beyond that market.
How many mystic martyrs

hidden in Love's soul
have abandoned the preacher's chair
to climb onto the scaffold!
Lovers who drink the wine's dregs
reel from bliss to bliss;
dark-hearted skeptics
burn inwardly with denial.
Intellect says, "Stay where you are!
Annihilation has only thorns!"
Love laughs, "The thorns are in you!"
Keep silent, and tear Being's thorn
out of your heart;
discover in your own soul
rose garden after rose garden.

For every house become a window,
for every field, a rose garden.
Run out of your self,
abandon your existence,
become Me without me.

Life of the Soul! Since you have a house
in every atom of this world,
why doesn't the dust of the road sing?
Why are stones shut down?
Why does poison kill?
Why do thorns pierce?
Why does anger flame into violence?
Why are nights black?
One morning in Your garden
I was amazed at how, during Your reign,
a thorn could still be a thorn.
"Has He," I thought, "out of self-jealousy,
masked His own face?
Does He sustain this 'distance'
so others cannot glimpse Him at all?
Or is it that the world's eye
is so cancered over and darkened,
it can see nothing, nothing at all,
of the tenderness of that radiant Face?"

You need fire and water for the fruit to ripen:
How can that occur without lightning and clouds?
Before the heart has shattered into lightning
and before rains of tears have fallen from your eyes,
how can the fire and menace of God's anger be appeased?
How could the green of the desire for Union grow?
How could the springs of limpid water start to flow?
How could the rosebuds whisper their secret to the garden?

How did my heart's rose

become this astounding red?

Through being washed again and again

in waves of bliss and blood.

In the driest
whitest stretch
of pain's
infinite desert
I lost my sanity
and found
this rose.

From what invisible rose garden
was flung this rose
whose perfume maddens
me and makes me lucid?

Blood must flow,
He said,
for the rose garden
to flower,
and the heart that
loves me
is a wound
without shield.

Make me sweet again,

fragrant and fresh and wild,

and thankful for any small gesture.

Set out now, while you're strong, on the heart's vast plain:
You'll never discover joy on the plain of the body.
The heart's the only house of safety, my friends:
It has fountains, and rose gardens within rose gardens.
Turn to the heart and go forward, travelers of the night;
there's where you'll find trees and streams of living water.

Like a pipe, I can say anything at all
when I'm joined, in harmony, with my Friend:
Separate from the one who speaks,
I grow silent, even if I know a hundred songs.
When the rose has gone and the garden faded,
you won't hear any more of the nightingale's story.
The Beloved is all that lives, the lover a dead thing.

My Face

is everywhere—

and

all you are

gazing at is

roses.

The whole world could be choked with thorns:
A lover's heart will stay a rose garden.
The wheel of heaven could wind to a halt:
The world of lovers will go on turning.
Even if every being grew sad, a lover's soul
will still stay fresh, vibrant, light.

You want to know
what these words
are like?
I am the rose bush of
Certainty's rose garden:
My words the fragrances
of its roses.

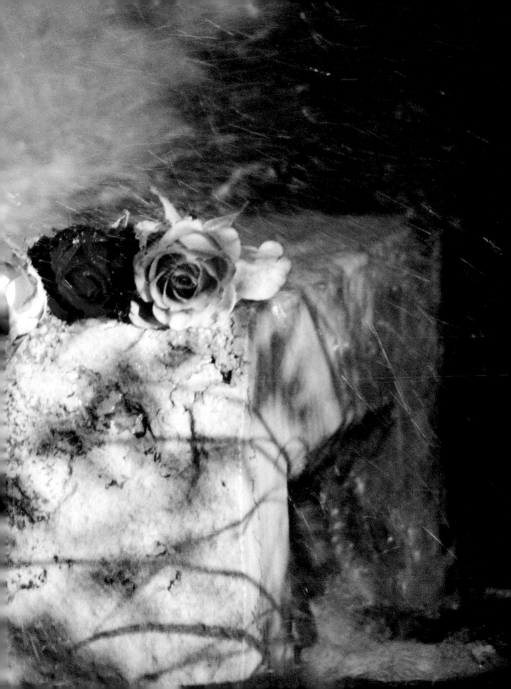

Stop learning.

Start knowing.

The rose opens, and opens,

and when it falls,

falls outward.

After despair, many hopes flourish
just as after rain
thousands of roses open.
Surrender to the Almighty—
and be led into life.

If you could see the ugliest leper with
the eyes of love,
his beauty would out-dazzle
the starlit sea.
If one drop of love's vision
could rinse your eyes,
wherever you looked, you would
weep with wonder.

Whatever your terror and
whatever the sacrifice,
grow the royal rose-heart
and step into the eternal garden.
For this dissolution you were created.
For this flowering beyond death
you were born.
Refuse this destiny,
and you refuse yourself yourself.

You thought that when your house
was burnt down
there would be nothing left but ash.
But look,
moonlight is dancing on white roses!

Don't be sad, my friend,
when the rose's petals all fall.
Seek the treasure of God
in the devastated heart.

My heart is like a vast rose garden of light.
An ocean of agony drowned it again and again
but it became a warrior
after being slaughtered a hundred times.

Could you ever find

another market like this?

Where with your one rose

you can buy thousands

of rose gardens

and with one final breath,

the Divine Wind?

Where would the full rose grow
but in rich dark dirt?
How but through love's agony
could you become love's timeless bliss?

If you want to know Him and yourself
look at this open rose—
from one infinite silent drunken heart
so many petals, so many worlds.

Ground yourself,
strip yourself down,
to blind loving silence.
Stay there, until you see
you are gazing at the rose
with its own ageless eyes.

Those tender words we said to one another
are stored in the secret heart of Heaven.
One day, like rain they will fall and spread
and their mystery will grow green over the world.

Freedom, your name is Love! Make me your slave!
Slavery to you is the door into the garden.
My door into eternity is exactly the shape I make
when I walk forward, head bowed, on my knees.

Breathe in the secret.

No more words.

Hear only the voice within.

Remember, the first thing

you said was:

We are beyond words.